George Colman, Joseph Atkinson

Tit for Tat

A Comedy in Three Acts

George Colman, Joseph Atkinson

Tit for Tat
A Comedy in Three Acts

ISBN/EAN: 9783744666473

Printed in Europe, USA, Canada, Australia, Japan

Cover: Foto ©Thomas Meinert / pixelio.de

More available books at **www.hansebooks.com**

TIT FOR TAT,

A

COMEDY

IN THREE ACTS.

Performed at the THEATRES ROYAL

HAY-MARKET,

DRURY-LANE, AND COVENT-GARDEN.

PRINTED UNDER THE INSPECTION OF
JAMES WRIGHTEN, PROMPTER.
EXACTLY AGREEABLE TO THE REPRESENTATION.

LONDON.
PRINTED FOR C. DILLY, IN THE POULTRY.
1788.

Dramatis Personæ.

HAY-MARKET, 1786.

VILLAMOUR,	MR. PALMER.
OLD MEANWELL,	MR. BOOTH.
YOUNG MEANWELL,	MR. DAVIES.
SKIPWELL,	MR. R. PALMER.
SERVANT,	MR. LYONS.
FLORINDA,	MISS FARREN.
LETTY,	MRS. BULKLEY.

TIT FOR TAT.

A COMEDY.

ACT I.

SCENE I. *An Apartment in Meanwell's House.*

OLD MEANWELL *discovered sitting (with a Letter in his Hand).*

THIS confidential information given me by *Villamour's* father puzzles me exceedingly; I don't know to act in it, whether 'tis better to forewarn my daughter of the plot meditated against her, or without assigning my motives, counsel her to turn his own weapons upon him?—the last seems to be the best method; but I will consult my son about it.——Oh; here comes Florinda and her confidante.

Enter Florinda and Letty.

FLORINDA.

What are your commands for me, Sir?

OLD MEANWELL.

I sent for you, my dear, to acquaint you, I've just received an account that Young *Villamour* will be here to-day: but you seem pensive and reserved.——Pray, child, don't be uneasy; come be *candid* with me, and you'll find me as indulgent as you could wish.

LETTY.

Why really, Sir, I was too precipitate in judging for

B   my my miſtreſs, ſhe's loth to riſk her heart in the lottery of love, with ſo many blanks to a prize.

OLD MEANWELL.

Come, come, this is not the point——I'll be plain with you, Florinda:—You muſt be ſenſible how dear you are to me—you know I told you before, that in the laſt excurſion I made to Ireland this buſineſs came on the tapis, his father and I agreed to the match, provided you ſhould mutually like each other, and that no compulſion was to be uſed on *either* ſide.

FLORINDA.

And yet, Sir, it is an aukward kind of interview at the beſt.

OLD MEANWELL.

I'll lay no injunction on your obedience to me ;—if *Villamour* does n't ſuit your inclinations, you need only ſay ſo, and the treaty's at an end ;——if *you* do not pleaſe his fancy, he'll depart immediately.

LETTY.

Yes, yes, quite like a ſoldier's courtſhip—you like me, I like you ; quick, let's be tether'd !——or do you like me ? No, nor I you ; ſo let's hear no more of it.

OLD MEANWELL.

I muſt confeſs, as I before told you, that I never ſaw *Villamour*; he was on his travels when I viſited his father— but from the character he bears, I dare ſay you'll join in my prepoſſeſſion for him, and have reaſon to thank us for bringing you together.

FLORINDA.

'I'm overpower'd with your goodneſs, Sir ; and ſince you throw implicit obedience out of the queſtion, I'll hazard the trial.

OLD MEANWELL.

You ſhall decide for yourſelf, Child, and be a free agent on this occaſion.

FLORINDA.

Then if I dare communicate a project that *Letty* here has ſtruck out for me—your compliance with it will entirely remove every apprehenſion. OLD

OLD MEANWELL.

Tell it me, if it is feasible I promise not only my consent, but assistance——

FLORINDA.

'Tis very feasible, Sir——but I am afraid it would be intruding too much on your indulgence.

OLD MEANWELL.

No——put it to the test, try me, one should be a little *too* good in this world to be *sufficiently* so.

FLORINDA.

None but the best of fathers and of men could utter that expression.

OLD MEANWELL.

Explain yourself, my dear.

FLORINDA.

Villamour, you say, is expected at our house to-day.—— If I could so manage it that we might be together without his knowing me, I should be quite easy;—*Letty* has presence of mind, and cleverness—will you consent to our interchanging characters, *she* to be mistress, and *I maid*.

LETTY.

And so make a gentlewoman of me in spite of the three penny planet I was born under;—rare work! nothing to do but drink tea, make curtesies, and get a husband!

OLD MEANWELL.

Odd enough, faith! the very thing I was going to propose to her.—(*Aside.*)

FLORINDA.

Well, Sir, have I your permission?

OLD MEANWELL.

Yes, my dear, I permit this metamorphosis, on condition you neither of you quit it, 'till I give you leave ——But will *Letty* be equal to *her* part of the drama?

LETTY.

Me, Sir, you know I'm an old spouter, and have done every character from *Cherry* to *Beatrice* at our holiday plays in the country. Observe the sample, and refuse me due respect if you dare?

" With a good leg and a good foot, Uncle, and money
" enough in his purse, such a man would win any

B 2

" woman

" woman in the world, if he could get her good
" will."

What do you think of me now, Sir, can you difcover a
trace of low life in your fervant Letty ?

OLD MEANWELL.

Hah! hah! hah! very well, very well, indeed ———
you'll be a capital performer: but there is no time to be
loft, go and equip yourfelves for your refpective parts ;—
make hafte, and tell the reft of the family to be on their
guard.

FLORINDA.

A very little alteration will anfwer my purpofe, for now
adays the maid is a finer lady than the miftrefs.

LETTY.

'But I muft to my toilet.——Come, Mrs. *Letty*, pray·
attend your duty, Ma'am, and make yourfelf a little handy
in your new employment.

FLORINDA.

You'll be fatisfied with my dutiful endeavours, Ma'am!
                  (Curtefying.)

As they are retiring, enter Young Meanwell.

YOUNG MEANWELL.

Sifter, I congratulate you ;—I've juft heard your lover
is expected here immediately.

FLORINDA.

I'm not your fifter at prefent;—pay your attention *there*,
if you pleafe ; but I haven't time to unravel the myftery
now, and fo leave my father to expound it.
            [*Exeunt Florinda and Letty.*

OLD MEANWELL.

Come, I'll tell you *more* than even fhe herfelf's *aware*
of, *Tom.*

YOUNG MEANWELL.

What I've already heard is enough to furprife me, Sir.

OLD MEANWELL.

But you muft be fecret ——Know then, when *Villamour*
comes here to-day, we fhall behold him in difguife.
                    YOUNG

YOUNG MEANWELL.

In difguife.——Is it from a mafquerade, or are you going to give him a fancy-ball at his reception?

OLD MEANWELL.

Neither;—but you muft know that his father has given me private notice, that *Villamour* (after much importunity) prevailed on him to permit his coming here in a fictitious character.

YOUNG MEANWELL.

How do you mean, Sir?

OLD MEANWELL.

You recollect that *Villamour* is ftill in the army, and that his old campaigner of a fervant ftill lives with him; and I am further to tell you, accompanies his mafter on the prefent occafion to London.——

YOUNG MEANWELL

And what of that pray?

OLD MEANWELL.

He, in *this* courtfhip, is to reprefent his mafter's name and character, while *Villamour* attends him in the double capacity of a private foldier, and valet, under his fervant's name, *Skipwell.*——

YOUNG MEANWELL.

What a romantic piece of knight errantry!

OLD MEANWELL.

And to compleat the jeft, *Florinda,* equally as uneafy refpecting the fight of her lover (whofe plot againft her fhe *can't* have a knowledge of (has juft implored me, that fhe and Letty fhould *likewife* make a mafquerade of it, by exchanging characters; and I've confented.——

YOUNG MEANWELL.

Oh that's a different ftory——I now fee 'twill produce a very original, comic adventure!.

OLD MEANWELL.

You would not advife me then to let your fifter know the counterplot againft her?——

YOUNG

YOUNG MEANWELL.

By no means, Sir, love feems to have contrived it, and let fortune have the management of it.——

Enter Florinda, dreffed as Letty.

FLORINDA.

Here I am, Sir——and what do you think of me? I'll endeavour to be as pert and faucy a waiting-maid as any in the precinéts of St. James's.

YOUNG MEANWELL.

If *Villamour's* fervant's as clever a fellow as we're told, and has but a good opinion of himfelf, indeed, Sifter, I think you'll be an excellent match for each other.

OLD MEANWELL.

As to that matter, if 'tis the fame perfon he had with him on his travels——I hear a good account of him, and that he's a very great favourite of his mafter's.

FLORINDA.

Well, for a little fport I fhould not be difpleafed to ftrike his fancy in the part I reprefent, but I fhould be more vain to be fure, if I could lure the notice of his mafter.—If I can but effeét a conqueft over him in this difguife, I fhall have a higher opinion of myfelf than ever.

OLD MEANWELL.

And fhe little knows what a good opportunity fhe'll have.
(Afide to Young Meanwell.)

FLORINDA.

As for the attendant his importunity will not much trouble me ;—there will be fomething commanding in my look and manner that will make him know his proper diftance, and the awful refpeét due to me.

YOUNG MEANWELL.

Not fo faft, Sifter, not fo faft; you muft confider this fellow will be *your equal.*

OLD MEANWELL.

And will not fail like the reft of them, to make downright *love* to you.

FLORINDA.

With all my heart; fervants are generally communicative ;

tive; love is a great babler, and foldier's always gallant ;
fo I'll make him the hiftorian of his mafter, and thus have
a better chance of unravelling his true character.

Enter a Servant.

Sir, there's a foldier below, juft arrived in town he
fays, who begs to fpeak with you.

OLD MEANWELL.

Shew him in.

[*Exit Servant.*

YOUNG MEANWELL.

I fuppofe 'tis Villamour's attendant coming to announce
his mafter.———Where's Letty ?

FLORINDA.

I left her at her toilet——where I dare fay her looking-
glafs flatters her that we are very imprudent to put *Villamour* in her power——but fhe'll be ready before he comes.

OLD MEANWELL.

O here's the *avant courier !*

*Enter a Servant, conducting Villamour difguifed in a Light
Infantry Uniform—as Skipwell.*

VILLAMOUR.

I was difpatched by my mafter, Mr. *Villamour*, to Mr.
Meanwell——Is it to him I have the honour of paying
my duty and refpects ?

FLORINDA.

If the mafter's but as fmart and well-looking as the fer-
vant---(*Afide.*)

OLD MEANWELL.

Yes, my friend, I'm the perfon you were fent to.

VILLAMOUR.

You have no doubt, Sir, been informed of our coming;
my mafter is dreffing at the hotel, and fent me before him
with his moft dutiful compliments 'till he confirms them
in perfon.

OLD MEANWELL.

And you execute your meffage in a very becoming manner ;

ner, don't you t! n k fo, *Letty ?* and that he's a good fore-
runner of his mafter?

FLORINDA.

I will not give my opinion too rafhlv, Sir.

YOUNG MEANWELL.

But you'll welcome the young man, won't you?

FLORINDA.

Certainly!——and what's more, I think he promffes
very well, Sir—

VILLAMOUR.

You do me honour in thinking fo:—I only wifh the
miftrefs half as charming as the maid.—(*Afide.*)

OLD MEANWELL.

But what's this fancy drefs you have got on ? Is it your
mafter's livery ?

VILLAMOUR.

Yes, Sir—and *one* that I prefer wearing to any other
livery in the world !

YOUNG MEANWELL.

Very heroic, indeed !—and well fpoken for a foldier of
light infantry.

OLD MEANWELL.

But can't your mafter travel without his body guard ?
that he will not let you equip yourfelf like every other *fervant.*

VILLAMOUR.

O, Sir, the hardfhips of war endear us foldiers to one
another, and we always regard our cloth too well, ever to
go on fervice, under falfe colours.

FLORINDA.

Then you look upon courtfhip as a kind of fervice ?

VILLAMOUR.

Certainly ! and the only one a foldier fears, becaufe the
moft fatal to his heart.

YOUNG MEANWELL.

Bravo !——he's quite Sterne's La Fleur ! take care of
your heart, my girl——for a faithful foldier always proves
himfelf a conftant lover.   FLORINDA.

FLORINDA.

My heart indeed !

VILLAMOUR.

Don't be offended ; what the gentleman's pleafed to fay will not make me prefume more on the poffibility of gaining it.

FLORINDA.

A modeft, pretty behaved fellow this:—(*Afide.*)

YOUNG MEANWELL.

This is mighty fine talk—but methinks it's a very ferious introduction for people of your clafs ;—fuch a grave formal manner don't fuit either of you :—you fhould be free and frolickfome as if acquainted for a month——This girl's name's *Letty*, what's your's my friend?

VILLAMOUR:

Skipwell, at your fervice, Sir.

OLD MEANWELL.

Come, *Tom*, we're only a reftraint on them.——Go, acquaint your fifter of Mr. *Villamour's* approach; and, *Letty*, do you fhew the young man his mafter's apartments; and I defire, my friend, that you'll take good care of yourfelf in this houfe.

VILLAMOUR.

Sir, you do me greater honour than I deferve.

[Exeunt Old and Young Meanwell.

(*After a Paufe*)——FLORINDA.

They're amufing themfelves at my expence——but I ca'nt help it——this lad feems neither ugly nor unpleafing; and I fhould not pity the fervant maid, that had him for a fweetheart.—-(*Afide*).

VILLAMOUR.

This girl aftonifhes me——there is not a rank in life that her figure and manners woudn't do honour to—— but I'll know more of her, and gain her confidence for my own fake—(*Afide*)   (*Addreffing himfelf to her*) Since we are now alone, on the friendly footing of fellowfervants, tell me, my dear, is your miftrefs as captivating as yourfelf?——At any rate fhe muft be exceedingly vain to venture on having an attendant like *you*.

C   FLORINDA.

FLORINDA.

The archnefs of this queftion is a direct proof that you've a great mind for a little flirtation with me?

VILLAMOUR.

To tell you the truth, I did not come to this houfe with any fuch intention:——for foldier as I am, I keep little company with fervants, I hate their low-liv'd wit, and the vulgarifm of their converfation.——

FLORINDA.

O, the precious coxcomb!—(*Afide*)

VILLAMOUR.

But with regard to you it is a different cafe——I was prepoffeffed in your favour the inftant I entered the room; and am inclined to treat you with the higheft refpect;—— then tell me what kind of a waiting·maid are you, with charms like a princefs?

FLORINDA.

What you have told me is exactly the language of all the *gentleman's fervants* that have feen me.——

VILLAMOUR.

And I fhould not be much furprifed if it was the opinion of all *their mafters.*

FLORINDA.

I thank you for that compliment, but I muft obferve to you that I'm never to be duped by the flatteries of their fervants·——

VILLAMOUR.

That is as much as to fay, that my ftation don't pleafe you.

FLORINDA.

True; for a fortune-teller once prophecied, that I fhould never marry any one but a gentleman of birth and fortune, and I have fince pofitively fwore never to accept any thing elfe.——

VILLAMOUR.

That's odd enough!——What you have refolved on refpecting a hufband, I have long determined on as to a wife, and made a folemn declaration never to marry any one but a gentlewoman.——

FLORINDA.

FLORINDA.

Then you need not folicit *me* I find.

VILLAMOUR.

I'm not fo much out in my purfuit as you perhaps imagine——*you* have a very genteel appearance! and one is often of a good family without knowing it.———

FLORINDA.

Hah! hah! hah!——I fhould thank you for that malicious compliment, if it was not at the expence of my mother.———

VILLAMOUR.

Revenge yourfelf on *mine* then, if you think I'm entitled to it.———

FLORINDA.

He really deferves it——(*Afide*)——But this is not the point, Mr. *Skipwell*, let us have done with this raillery, a man of wealth and fashion is what I afpire to, and I'll not give up a tittle of it.

VILLAMOUR.

Egad! had I the good fortune to have-been born fuch, I fhould verify the fortune-teller's prediction.

FLORINDA.

Come, come, this is too much——I defire once more you'll quit this topic.

VILLAMOUR.

You muft throw away your charms then.

FLORINDA.

You will not have done then——I muft leave you——I really fhould have done fo before——(*Afide*——*going*)

VILLAMOUR.

Stay one moment if you pleafe——I had fomething particular to afk *you*, but it's gone quite out of my head.

FLORINDA (*returning*).

I too had fomething to fay to *you*, but you have confufed me fo!——

VILLAMOUR.

O: now I remember afking you, if your miftrefs was as pleafing as yourfelf.

C 2   FLORINDA.

FLORINDA.

This is only returning to the old fubject.

VILLAMOUR.

Oh, no fair Lititia!—*this* merely concerns my mafter,

FLORINDA.

It was relative to him too that *I* wifhed to fpeak ;——
tell me candidly what fort of a man he is; *your* attachment
gives me a good opinion of him ; he muft have fome merit when *you* ferve him.

VILLAMOUR.

You can't refufe me thanking you for that flattering
compliment however.

FLORINDA.

Don't take notice of it——it was faid inadvertently,
and can't be recalled.

VILLAMOUR.

There again is one of thofe cold cruel anfwers that
chill me——but do what you pleafe, I have only to regret
that fortune has not allotted me a ftation worthy of you.

FLORINDA.

——Let's have no more of this nonfenfe——O here's
your mafter come at laft ; I muft ftay and have a peep at
him.

Enter Skipwell (dreffed in an Officer's Uniform.)

SKIPWELL.

Ah! *Skipwell,* are you there?——well, were my bag-
gage and you gracioufly received?

VILLAMOUR.

It was impoffible it could be otherwife, Sir.

SKIPWELL.

Go, and acquaint my father-in-law and my *wife* of my
arrival.

FLORINDA.

What a difagreeable fellow.—(*Afide.*)—I fuppofe you
mean Mr. *Meanwell* and his daughter, Sir.

SKIPWELL.

Yes, my wife and father-in-law, 'tis the fame thing,
isn't it, child? I'm come to be married, and they expect me
for

for that purpofe ; don't they ? It wants nothing but the ceremony, and that's a trifle.

FLORINDA.

'Tis a trifle however requiring fome ferious confideration, Sir——

SKIPWELL.

Perhaps fo ; but the more one thinks of it, the lefs they'll like it, ' too much pudding will choak a dog.'

VILLAMOUR.

Oh ! curfe your proverbs ; I wifh they'd choak *you*— [*Afide*]

FLORINDA.

I fee that fenfe and merit are at a very cheap rate in your country—[*Afide to Villamour.*]

SKIPWELL.

What are you faying to my fervant-man, girl ?

FLORINDA.

Nothing, Sir——but——that I wonder what keeps my mafter.

SKIPWELL.

Why not my father-in-law, pray ?

FLORINDA.

Becaufe he is not yet fo.

VILLAMOUR.

Certainly not, Sir, 'till the nuptials are accomplifhed.

SKIPWELL.

O, langolee for ever !——I'm ready in a crack——and fo is the Lady, I'll be bail for her.

FLORINDA.

Oh ! the vulgar wretch—[*Afide*]—but we- muft firft dance at your wedding, Sir—and get gloves and *favours*.

SKIPWELL.

And was any of my country ever backwards at a wedding!—though we often get only black eyes for *favours*— and fo call my father-in-law, pray !

VILLAMOUR.

Was there ever fuch an ignorant provoking rafcal ?—— [*Afide*]

FLORINDA.

14   TIT FOR TAT,

FLORINDA.

You are in great haste to be married, Sir, though for
what *you* know my miſtreſs may be a great coquette, or
an arrant ſcold!

SKIPWELL.

That won't frighten me;—a man living in a barrack
iṣ ſoon uſed to the clatter of the drums, and may lie cloſe
to a church *ſteeple*, without being diſturbed by the *bells*.

FLORINDA.

What delicate ſentiments!—[*Aſide*]—You ſpeak quite
like a *philoſopher*, Sir.

SKIPWELL.

O, yes, very like a FIELD OFFICER.

VILLAMOUR.

Was there ever ſuch an infernal blunderer?—*(Aſide)*

SKIPWELL.

But harky'e, my girl; are you my Lady'ṣ waiting-
maid *here*, and ſingle, I preſume by your innocence?——
She's a mighty fine girl, upon my honour!

FLORINDA.

Both, Sir——but not at *your* ſervice.—*(Aſide)*

SKIPWELL.

Well, how do you like me? Don't you think I ſhall
prove very agreeable here.

FLORINDA.

O! *mighty* agreeable! *very* agreeable indeed, Sir!

SKIPWELL.

That's well; encourage that notion, it may be ſervice-
able to yourſelf, my dear, in the end——She's a nice
tit.——

FLORINDA.

Well, Sir, I'll go acquaint my maſter that you're come;
they certainly muſt have forgot to tell him.——Capricious
fate! were ever two men ſo miſplaced in life—*(Aſide)*

[*Exit Florinda.*

SKIPWELL.

Well, Sir, *you* ſee the beginning of the plot goes off
very well——I already prove agreable, and have made
my way with the prime miniſter.

VILLAMOUR.

VILLAMOUR.

You ill-manner'd, incorrigible blockhead!

SKIPWELL.

What, Sir, with fo pleafing an addrefs! fo genteel an air as mine!—(*Looking at himfelf*)

VILLAMOUR.

After all the inftructions I give you, to behave with fuch ignorance and vulgarity!—I particularly defired you to be referved and fedate; to hide your brogue, and avoid proverbs!

SKIPWELL.

Then you would have me as mute as a fifh, and not fay word. Confider, Sir, I have not been long a gentleman, but I'll improve by practice; and fince I have not gravity enongh for you, in future I'll be quite fad, and cry my eyes out, if you chufe it, Sir.

VILLAMOUR.

I do not know what to think, fay, or do——I'm quite embaraffed——I wifh I had never undertaken this adventure.

SKIPWELL.

Why, Sir, does not the lady fuit your *palate?*

VILLAMOUR.

Silence;——here's fomebody coming——O! it is Mr. *Meanwell,* fo mind my advice, *deport* yourfelf properly; and if he afks you about *Ireland,* do not forget the leffon I gave you, particularly *the fpeech.——*

SKIPWELL.

Mum!——never fear, Sir;——I'll *report* myfelf properly.   [*Exit Villamour.*

Enter Old Meanwell.

OLD MEANWELL.

My dear Mr. *Villamour,* I afk you a thoufand pardons for having been out of the way on your arrival.

SKIPWELL.

A thoufand pardons, Sir——if they came from *Rome,* are quite too many——*one* is fufficient for one *omiffion;*—but if I had a million, they fhould be at your fervice.

OLD

OLD MEANWELL.

I hope I shall not have occasion for any *more*, Sir. But I'm quite rejoiced to see you here, Sir; I hope you left my good old friend, your father, perfectly well, Sir.

SKIPWELL.

Never better, Sir, never better, and always at your service.

OLD MEANWELL.

So, I find you could not resist visiting your Dear Hibernia, before your regiment and your mistress; you longed, I suppose, to behold the many happy changes that she had experienced in your absence.

SKIPWELL.

Yes, Sir——now for the speech—*(Aside)*—and was rejoiced to 'find my country as free in her commerce and constitution as England——with equal prospects of wealth, fame, and prosperity before her——as my master says——

OLD MEANWELL.

Your master!

SKIPWELL.

O curse my blundering tongue—*(Aside)*—Master!—did I say Master?——O yes, the *Quarter-Master* of our regiment, a staff-officer, Sir——And—and as great a politician as I am ——Hem! to be sure I an't the dandy—
Aside)

OLD MEANWELL.

O, your humble servant, Sir!——well recovered, faith! —*(Aside)*—However we will defer politics 'till we are over the bottle.

SKIPWELL.

O yes——politics is a *dry* subject sure enough.

OLD MEANWELL.

Well, Sir, how do you like the continent and the courts you've seen in your travels.

SKIPWELL.

O vastly well, Sir——I learned to caper and take snuff in France;——the art of war and drinking in Germany; ——to be sulky and proud as a grandee, in Spain.——to sing and play the fiddle in Italy;——and among the
Turks

Turks to chew opium like bacce ;——as to *learning* and
good manners, they're quite natural to me.

OLD MEANWELL.

Very great accomplifhments indeed!

SKIPWELL.

But I'm vaftly impatient to fee your fair daughter, Sir
and have been equiping and *adamizing* myfelf as you fee
to win her——

OLD MEANWELL.

Hah! hah! hah!—(*Afide*)—*you* judged well, the drefs
recommends the wearer, and " the brave deferve the fair."

SKIPWELL.

But when fhall I fee her, Sir ?

OLD MEANWELL.

Oh : immediately !—She has not been very well, *rather*
——a *little agitated*—expecting *you.*

SKIPWELL.

Oh! dear Sir——

OLD MEANWELL.

The bafhfulnefs of a *maid* you know !——In the mean
time, will you take any refrefhment after your journey ?

SKIPWELL.

" Will a duck fwim ?"——I never refufes to crack a
bottle with an honeft fellow, for I love to wet my whiftle.

OLD MEANWELL.

It's rather early for drinking, but the houfe and cellar
are both at your fervice.

SKIPWELL.

For my part I'll be content with the cellar.

OLD MEANWELL.

Pray, Sir.

SKIPWELL.

Oh! not for the world——I'll follow you, Sir——

OLD MEANWELL.

Well, Sir, I'll fhew the way.——*Exit.*

D

SKIPWELL.

If I'm not as polite, and as much a gentleman as my
master, the devil burn me.

(*Exit.*

E N D O F A C T I.

A C T   II.

S C E N E I   *Meanwell's Houfe.*

Old Meanwell, and Letty drefs'd as Florinda.

OLD MEANWELL.

WELL, Letty, I fee you are drefs'd for your character——what have you to fay to me?

LETTY.

Sir, fomething very particular to communicate to you.

OLD MEANWELL.

Ah! what is it?

LETTY.

To clear up matters, that you may have nothing to re-
proach me with hereafter.

OLD MEANWELL.

You're very ferious I find.

LETTY.

Very ferious I affure you, Sir——I readily became an
accomplice in the plot, not imagining any confequence
from it to myfelf.

OLD MEANWELL.

Why, what mighty confequence has happened to you?

LETTY.

'Tis a bold tafk to praife one's felf; but in fpite of all
the rules of modefty, I muft inform you, Sir, that if you
do

do not reveal matters, your intended fon-in-law won't have
a heart to give my miftrefs——It is time the mafk was
thrown off, and that he fhould know who is who——elfe
I cannot be anfwerable for it a day longer.

OLD MEANWELL.

And what makes you imagine he will not admire my
daughter when he comes to a thorough knowledge of her?
——Have *you* any doubt of her charms, pray?

LETTY.

By no means, Sir, but you have no opinion of mine—
I forwarn you however that they are doing great execution
——and I advife you to guard againft them.

OLD MEANWELL.

O, Ma'am, I beg you a thoufand pardons, I was not
acquainted with your powers, Hah! hah! hah!

LETTY.

Very well, Sir, laugh as much as you pleafe; but believe
me I'm right, and I can gain my point if I chufe it.

OLD MEANWELL.

Very well, Letty, do fo, *I* fhall not hinder you affure
yourfelf.

LETTY.

I muft be more explicit, Sir——Mr. Villamour's heart is
going very faft; Ive already won it.——I know I am not
deferving of it——he'll have a wretched tafte, and all
that——

OLD MEANWELL.

O, by no means——you are too humble indeed.

LETTY.

You may conceive whatever you pleafe, Sir; but——
mind what I tell you, Sir, by to-morrow he'll be entirely
in my leading-ftrings.

OLD MEANWELL.

With all my heart, if he loves you fo defperately let
him marry you.

LETTY.

What——and you'll not forbid the banns, Sir.

D 2   OLD

Old Meanwell.

Not I, upon my honour, if you can bring *him* to it.

Letty.

Once more I warn you to take care, Sir——I have not yet given full fcope to my powers, but if I am permitted to difplay myfelf, and at liberty to exert all the arts of my fex, I'll conquer all before me.

Old Meanwell.

Conquer, captivate, fink, burn and deftroy—in fhort— marry him, I give you full permiffion and confent.

Letty.

Then, Sir, I thank you, and confider my fortune as already made.

Old Meanwell.

But here comes ' your conquering hero.'

Enter Skipwell.

Skipwell.

Ah! have I at length found you, my enchanting fair one? I have been hunting all round the houfe for you, like a young hound after a liveret, as I'm not happy a minute from your fight——your fervant, father-in-law that is to be——

Old Meanwell.

Good bye, my children; a third perfon on thefe occafions is not the moft acceptable company——So I will leave you to yourfelves——' Love firft and marry afterwards.'

Skipwell.

I'm glad, Sir, you have reverfed the proverb, but I can do thofe *two* things both together.

Old Meanwell.

Have a little patience, do not hurry my daughter's fpirits, her *nerves* are very delicate.   [*Exit.*

Skipwell.

Yes, fomething like *fiddle-ftrings*——they will bear playing upon——How much at his eafe the old gentleman talks, and how quietly he bids us have patience.

Letty,

LETTY.

And can I believe, Sir, you are such an enemy to delay? It is certainly your politenefs and gallantry make you
fay fo; for I am but juft known to you; your love cannot
have grown to fuch a pitch already; I may fay it is but
newly born.

SKIPWELL.

You're miftaken, fair lady——a love of your making
fprouts up all at once like a *mufhroom*.——The firft ogle
from the *gable-end* of your bright eye made him a fine,
jolly, amorous, full-grown Cupid — like Cupid in the pict-
ure at Rome——Ah! make much of him then, fince you
are Venus the mother of him.

LETTY.

How much like a lover and a *traveller* he talks—(*Afide*)
You cannot fay, Sir, that he has been cruelly treated,
though he is a bold, impudent fellow, you muft own.

SKIPWELL.

'Till he is better provided for, give him then this
pretty, little, white hand of yours for a play thing to amufe
the child—" When the cat's away the mice will play."

LETTY.

There then, you little coaxing, enticing, pleafing rogue,
you, fince I cannot quiet you any other way.
(*Giving him her hand.*

SKIPWELL.

Dear, fweet, charming fugar candy of my heart, how
it fires me like—a fquib of whifkey! (*Kiffing it;*

LETTY.

How familiar and complaifant—(*Afide*)—Stop, ftop, you
are too greedy——do not take it for a gingerbread baby,
or think that you are fucking a China orange.

SKIPWELL.

Oh! it has fuch a relifh I could devour it, thumb, fingers
and all.

LETTY.

Is it poffible you can love me to fuch excefs——I can
hardly believe the reality of it;

SKIP-

SKIPWELL.

Talk not to me of what's poffible ; I love you to——
What the devil fhall I fay—(*Afide*) to *botheration* ; and
you know I do———

LETTY.

Oh ; there's no refifting you *red coats*——But hift—
here is fome body coming——Oh, it is *your* fervant.

Enter Villamour.

VILLAMOUR.

May I be allowed the liberty of fpeaking to you, Sir ?

SKIPWELL.

No ;—curs'd be the puppy that dare intrude on our
privacy, and interrupt our converfation——Begone, Sir,
or elfe———

VILLAMOUR.

I have not above a word or two to fay, Sir.

SKIPWELL.

Excufe me, Ma'am, if he utters above two *money fyllabubs* the third fhall be his difcharge.

VILLAMOUR.

Oh, damn your fyllabubs——Come here, firrah, ungra-
cious dunderhead, come near—(*Afide.*)

SKIPWELL.

Fine ufage for an officer, and a gentleman this—(*Afide
to Villamour*)---Come, difpatch, or I'll trounce your
jacket—Excufe me, my queen.

LETTY.

Ufe no ceremony with me, fir, finifh your bufinefs——

VILLAMOUR.

Hear me, you fcaramouch, difengage yourfelf from all
this mummery—do not give into it ; appear very ferious
and diffatisfied—nay, out of humour—you underftand
me. (*Afide to Skipwell.*)

SKIPWELL.

Mum—(*Afide*)—it is very well, let him call to morrow
or this evening——if you chufe, Ma'am———Go, firrah,
and tell him fo.   [*Exit Villamour.*

LETTY.

LETTY.

Pray who is it, fir?

SKIPWELL.

Oh, *no body*, Ma'am, fome fnip of a taylor, about wedding cloaths, that's all———a plague on the impertinence of fervants.

LETTY.

They are very troublefome indeed, Sir.

SKIPWELL.

Oh! Ma'am, but for this intrufion, I had fuch tender things to fay to you—But I can only remember what is uppermoft in my heart—that I love you, and hope I may expect a mutual return!

LETTY.

'Tis a kind of a fudden---unexpected---queftion, fir ;--. but---*you* may live in hopes---(*Affectedly*)

SKIPWELL.

Do you think then you could make a little hole in your heart for me to creep in at---(*Languifhing*)

LETTY.

Oh! now you are too coaxing, fir, confider the decorum of my fex———you have too much tinder and touchwood about you, and have not patience to raife a flame.

SKIPWELL.

Let me firft light up a match———You will be the flint, I the fteel, and fo we'll ftrike up a flafh of love between us!

LETTY.

But what would you have me fay, Sir?

SKIPWELL.

Only that you love me---be merely my echo, and repeat my words, my princefs.

LETTY.

You are very preffing, fir———Well, I believe *I love* you, fir.———(*Holding up her fan*)

SKIPWELL.

Oh, my dear little jewel --how you tranfport me--- I fhall die with joy---I'll not let you fay another word, but feal up your lips with mine---(*Kifsing her.*)

LETTY.

LETTY.

Oh, fye, fir---Perhaps when you know *me* thoroughly, you will love me lefs.

SKIPWELL.

Ah, Ma'am, when it comes to *that* you'll be the great-eft *lofer*, " and find yourfelf in the wrong box."

LETTY.

You do not know *what kind of a woman I am*, fir ; *I am* not fo *worthy* of you as you think me.

SKIPWELL.

And I fhould be on my knees when *I* fpeak to *you*, Ma'am.

LETTY.

As to *me* I fhould have chofen *you* in any ftation. Can I flatter myfelf that you'd be as kind to me ?

SKIPWELL.

Ah, my darling, were you only the flea-catcher of a lady's lap dog, or that I faw you with the proker in your hand making the kitchen fire, I would kneel to *that* as my fceptre, and obey you ; that I would, my Queen of Hearts.

LETTY.

I fhall foon put that to the teft (*Aside*) If I could be fure that your love was fincere.

SKIPWELL.

. Let us then fwear to be true and faithful to each other, in fpite of all the chances and chequers of this mortal life.

LETTY.

With all hearts——(*They both drop on their knees together*) Hear us, O Mafter Cupid.

SKIPWELL.

And *Cymon*, God of Marriage.

LETTY.

Who?

SKIPWELL.

Cymon.

LETTY.

Hymen *you* mean.

SKIPWELL.

SKIPWELL.

True, *he was* a High-man fure enough!

LETTY.

Hear our vows, that we will ever love and take each other for better for worfe——though fortune fhould betray our hopes and make beggars of either, or both of us.

SKIPWELL.

And I confent with all my foul——and now let's fign and feal the bargain—(*Kiffing her.*)

(*They both rife.*)

LETTY.

That feals the deed with a witnefs——and now——but here's another coming to interrupt us——Hufh!

Enter Florinda.

LETTY.

What do you want, Letty?

FLORINDA.

A meffage, to you, Ma'am.

SKIPWELL.

Muft we always be the flaves of fervants——you fee we are bufy, my child; cannot you come again? *Filly de Chambers* fhould not intrude, but when they are called for.

FLORINDA.

I've private bufinefs with my Lady, Sir.

LETTY.

Can't you put it off?

FLORINDA.

Why, really——Ma'am——

SKIPWELL.

Curfe that——*Why*——it throws me into the dumps;——I tell you, girl, *your abfence would be very good company.*

FLORINDA.

Oh! the difagreeable wretch—(*Aside*)—It is very urgent, Ma'am.

LETTY.

Then, fir, with your leave——

E SKIPWELL.

SKIPWELL.

If it muſt be ſo, it muſt ; then adieu, my deareſt honey.
(*Looking tenderly at each other.*)

[*Exeunt Florinda and Letty.*

Manet SKIPWELL.

This is all mighty fine——but ſhan't I be guilty of diſ-
obedience of orders in betraying my maſter ?——No——
he has tranſmogrified me into a gentleman ; at leaſt the
repreſentative of one ;---and I am not the *firſt repreſentative that has betrayed his truſt.*   [*Exit.*

Scene changes to another Apartment.

Enter Florinda and Letty.

FLORINDA.

You juſt behaved as I wiſhed you, Letty, not to ſend
away that deteſtable fellow, 'till I became a witneſs to his
vulgarity and ill-breeding.

LETTY.

Upon my word, Ma'am, it is too much for me to play
two parts at once——I muſt either be miſtreſs or maid, to
command or obey.

FLORINDA.

Well, but ſince he is not preſent, liſten to me as your
ſuperior——You plainly ſee that he is not agreeable to me.

LETTY.

You have not had time to examine him, Ma'am.

FLORINDA.

Is it neceſſary to ſee him above twice?——I tell you
again he will not anſwer my purpoſe.

LETTY

But he will mine though—(*Aſide*)—Perhaps your father
thinks otherwiſe, Ma'am.

FLORINDA.

It may be ſo, for he avoids meeting me ; nor have I
exchanged a ſyllable with him ſince Villamour's arrival—
Thus circumſtanced, it is only you, Letty, that can extri-
cate me from this troubleſome affair, by telling the gentleman that he does not ſuit your taſte.

LETTY.

LETTY.

I cannot indeed, Ma'am.

FLORINDA.

You *cannot* truly!——Pray what hinders you?

LETTY

Your father.

FLORINDA.

He prevent you; that is impoffible.

LETTY.

Pofitively forbade me, Ma'am.

FLORINDA.

Well, it is my orders you acquaint him that my diftafte to this gentleman is invincible; and I cannot think, after what he promifed, that he'll deceive me by detaining Villamour.

LETTY.

Has not his coxcomb of a fkip prejudiced you againft him by fome ftories to his difadvantage?

FLORINDA.

Pray, Ma'am, who gave you liberty to abufe any one? ——What could his fervant fay to difguft me more than his own ill-manners.

LETTY.

I however miftruft that you liften too much to this prating jackanapes of a foldier—who gives himfelf airs becaufe he meets encouragement; I fuppofe—(*Saucily*)

FLORINDA.

I muft once more defire that you will behave yourfelf refpectfully; the young man is very difcreet, fenfible and deferving.

LETTY.

Yes, yes, Ma'am, he's a very good flirt, and has art enough to prejudice people in his favour.

FLORINDA.

But I defire you'll not impute to the fervant the fixed abhorrence I bear the mafter.

LETTY.

Oh! Ma'am, fince you take his part, I will not offend you by faying any thing to his difadvantage.

E 2   FLORINDA·

FLORINDA.

I take his part——I juſtify him——*(fluttered)*

LETTY.

Indeed, Ma'am, you ſeem to entertain a very favourable kind of opinion of him.

FLORINDA.

I a favourable—*I* a kind opinion of him ——what inſolence ! you abſolutely loſe all reſpect for me, and fancy yourſelf, I believe, miſtreſs in reality.

LETTY.

I am ſorry that ſuch a trifle ſhould offend you, Ma'am.

FLORINDA.

Get out of my ſight——I'll take other meaſures to diſengage myſelf from this vexatious buſineſs.

[*Exit Letty.*

Manet FLORINDA.

I tremble at the bare thoughts of her ſuggeſtion—— How inſolently ſervants behave when we put ourſelves in their power, and are indiſcreet enongh to truſt them with our ſecrets ! I am vexed at what ſhe ſaid—it was relative to a ſervant ;—well, poor fellow, it is not his fault, and I ſhould not vent my diſpleaſure on him——but I ſee him yonder muſing and diſturbed——it will only diſtreſs me to meet him—ſo I will avoid him. (*going.*)

Enter Villamour.

VILLAMOUR.

Stay : Are you avoiding me, fair Letitia? What have I done to offend you ? Believe me, for the ſhort time we have to be together, you need not put yourſelf under any reſtraint.

FLORINDA.

What ! is your maſter going to leave us ? We ſhall not have much loſs of *him.*

VILLAMOUR.

Nor of *me* neither ; I have finiſhed your ſentence, have not I, Letty ?

FLORINDA.

I would not have tacked that to it, as I was not thinking of you.

VILLAMOUR.

VILLAMÓUR.

And I never lofe fight of you.

FLORINDA.

Hear me once for all, Skipwell—*go, come, or ſtay*, are equally indifferent to me——I neither like you, nor diſlike you, nor will I ever change this difpoſition——I have particular reaſons for it, and indeed I might excufe myſelf from telling you ſo.

VILLAMOUR.

Nay, now you make me miſerable——if piquing my pride was out of the queſtion, I ſhould be made wretched by your indifference. If you felt but half of what I ſuffer— and what an extraordinary ſituation I am in.

FLORINDA.

As to that it cannot be more embarraſſed than mine, I aſſure you——But I hope *you* are not going to leave us in reality.

VILLAMOUR.

Yes, I muſt go, or loſe my ſenſes, as I have already done my heart—and I was to blame in not leaving you the inſtant I ſaw you.

FLORINDA.

You cannot ſay that ever I encouraged your paſſion.

VILLAMOUR.

But you cannot hinder me from adoring you, and on my knees, I muſt confeſs my love—though I leave you the moment after.

(*As he is kneeling, Old and Young Meanwell enter at the back Scene, liſtening.*)

VILLAMOUR.

But before I riſe, ah! give me ſome aſſurance that I am not an object of your hatred.

FLORINDA.

Riſe, riſe, ſome body may catch you in this poſture ——do, I befeech you riſe——I'll ſay any thing you pleaſe ——I do not hate you, I aſſure you I do not.

VILLAMOUR,

VILLAMOUR.
What, Letty, if I was not what I appear to be, but a
man of family and fortune, and that I loved you as much
as I do now, you would have no diflike to me?

FLORINDA.
I fhould be a fool if I had.

VILLAMOUR.
You would return me love for love.

FLORINDA.
I fhould return you——(*Seeing her father and brother
coming*).

OLD MEANWELL.
A very tender, amorous duetto indeed!—What a pity
it is to interrupt fuch a pair of cooing doves.

FLORINDA.
This compleats my confufion—(*Afide*—)Could I hinder
the man going on his knees, Sir?

YOUNG MEANWELL,
Not if he was faying his prayers to you, Letty!

OLD MEANWELL.
I have fomething to fay to you in private, girl—with
that gentleman's leave;—you can at any time renew your
converfation.

VILLAMOUR.
I was juft going as you came in, Sir.

YOUNG MEANWELL.
O yes, like a pilgrim to his faint—we faw you on your
knees.

OLD MEANWELL.
Go then, and behave with more refpect to your mafter
than it is faid you do.

VILLAMOUR.
Me, Sir.

YOUNG MEANWELL.
Yes, *you*, Sir; we hear ftrange ftories of your ingrati-
tude, and mifreprefentation of him——*this* damfel is in
your confidence I find——

VILLAMOUR.
I do not know what you mean, Sir.

OLD MEANWELL.

A C O M E D Y.

Old Meanwell.
You may retire, and juſtify yourſelf another time.

Villamour.
Damnation! muſt I ſuffer this.——Oh cruel diſguiſe, that ſubjects me to ſuch painful reſtraint and indignity—— (*Aſide*)　　　　　　　　　　　　　　*Exit Villamour.*

(*Florinda walks about diſcompoſed.*)

Young Meanwell.
There muſt be ſomething, dear ſiſter, there muſt be ſomething in this ——

Florinda.
In *your* head, brother——but nothing in mine——except amazement at your queſtions and ſuſpicions.

Young Meanwell.
Did not I tell you this ſpark would make love to you?

Old Meanwell.
Come, come, it is this mighty ſoldier that has given you an antipathy to his maſter.

Florinda.
Pray, was it that audacious mock gentlewoman, Mrs. Letty, told you ſo?

Young Meanwell.
No indeed, it is evident from your own behaviour, which has become very teſty and captious of late.

Florinda.
Becauſe I am quite ſick of this fooliſh farce, and would have thrown off my diſguiſe before now, had I my father's permiſſion.

Old Meanwell.
I cannot at preſent indulge you, and as I agreed to it to humour you, you muſt pleaſe me by wearing it a little longer.

Florinda.
If I do, it is very reluctantly, ſir;—but I muſt aſſure you Villamour's ſervant is not at all blameable in this affair.

Young

Young Meanwell.

Well, there is but one way of fettli ng it to the fatisfaction of all parties——Skipwell is fufpected, fo we will per-
fuade his mafter to difcharge him——Do not you think it
is the beft method, fifter ?—(*Archly*)

Florinda.

O certainly ; and if that is done I muft likewife defire
Mrs. Letty not to come near me—I hate *her* even more
than Villamour.

Old Meanwell.

Do not be fo prejudiced, my dear ; fufpend your judg-
ment 'till you know him better——I'll anfwer for it, *Villamour* is the man of your choice at laft.

Florinda.

Will not you allow me to have eyes, to have ears, fir ;
I have already heard and feen enough of him to deteft him.

Young Meanwell.

In fpite of this, I'll lay any wager that you'll marry Villamour, and with your own confent——but I muft inter-
ceed for *Skipwell*, and beg you will forgive him, fir.

Florinda.

As he has not offended us, we have no right to be angry
with him.

Young Meanwell.

Then. fince he " *fo teizes and he fo pleafes*"—my fifter,
to oblige *her*, father.

Old Meanwell.

We will leave him to his mafter.

Florinda.

Well, brother, fince you will not leave off amnfing
yourfelf at my expence——I'll no longer pay for the entertainment ; fo good bye, Mr. Banter.

[*Exit.*

Old and Young Meanwell.

Hah ! hah ! hah !

Old Meanwell.

Well, I think, Tom, by the time the piece is conclu-
ded, they will both have reafon to be heartily tired of their
characters, and fufficiently punifhed for the plot contrived
againft each other.   [*Exeunt.*

END OF ACT II.

A C T III.

Scene an Apartment in Meanwell's House.

Enter Villamour and Skipwell.

SKIPWELL.

Ah! good Sir, my moſt honoured maſter——I beg of
you ——

VILLAMOUR.

You impudent double-faced impoſtor.

SKIPWELL.

O, Sir, do not take the game out of my hand when I
am going to muzzle it——Do not ſtop me when I am juſt
entering the goal—be compaſſionate to an old faithful ſervant, whoſe fortune entirely depends on your ſecrecy.

VILLAMOUR.

A raſcal to think——

SKIPWELL.

All true, Sir——but I am not the *firſt raſcal* who has
made his fortune.

VILLAMOUR.

What! would you have me let a worthy man be co-
zened by your tricks, and his family deceived under my
name and character? Would you diſgrace *your country*,
you dog, you?

SKIPWELL.

Ah! Sir, what is a man's *country* to *his own* intereſt ?

VILLAMOUR.

If you never mention it again, the inſtant I have diſco-
vered you to the family, I will have you diſmantled of
your robes, and put in the pillory.

SKIPWELL.

But liſten to me, Sir——this dear girl adores me——
loves me as a kitten does cream——If I acquaint her of my
ſtation, and that ſhe ſtill ſhould have a liquoriſh-tooth for
a healthy, clever, tight fellow like me—though not a gentleman——

VILLAMOUR.

Oh! if they once know you they may do as they pleaſe
——I waſh my hands of it.

F

SKIP.

SKIPWELL.

Then I'll immediately go and difcover myfelf to the tender-hearted generous lady, unplume myfelf of lace and feathers, and convince you that it is not the colour or quality of a coat, nor all your borrowed finery, that can make any difference in her love, and as Mr. Homer fays, in Pope's *Eye-lids,*

"When great *Ulyffes*——

VILLAMOUR.

The fellow's in heroics.

SKIPWLL.

You will fee what I am able to do in *paupere perfonis,* as we fay in Latin——and depend upon it that from carrying Brown Befs I fhall carry Madam Florinda, and have clevernefs enough, from waiting at the fide-board, to fit at the table; and that inftead of jolting *behind* the coach, become an agreeable companion in a poft-chaife.

[*Exit.*

VILLAMOUR.

All that paffes here is like a dream——it is fcarcely eredible——but I wifh I could fee Letty, perhaps by difcovering myfelf to her, fhe could relieve me from this embaraffment; and yet to *leave her* would be the greateft misfortune of all!——I'll fee if I can find her——Ah! fhe's here.

Enter Florinda.

VILLAMOUR,

I was in fearch of you, Letty.

FLORINDA.

It was hard to find me, for I have loft myfelf—(*Going.*)

VILLAMOUR (*Stopping her.*)

Stay, I conjure you, ftay, this is the laft time I fhall trouble you——it is on a matter of the greateft confequence to your miftrefs and the honour of the family.

FLORINDA.

Tell it to themfelves then——I never fee you, or hear you, but you give me fome caufe of uneafinefs.

VIL,

VILLAMOUR.

You have the same effect on me——but know, that matters will now wear different face from what they have heretofore done.

FLORINDA.

Well since you raise my curiosity, I'll hear you *this* once, and *this time* only.

VILLAMOUR.

But will you promise to be secret?

FLORINDA.

I never yet betrayed any one.

VILLAMOUR.

You only owe the confidence I am going to place in *you* to the esteem I bear you.

FLORINDA.

Never mind the motive, but trust my fidelity and believe me.

VILLAMOUR.

Then know, that the man now speaking to you is not what *he* seems.

FLORINDA.

What are you then?—(*Impatient*)

VILLAMOUR.

O, Letty, now is your time to triumph——Is there any one coming?

FLORINDA:

No——

VILLAMOUR.

The situation things are in forces me to this discovery.

FLORINDA.

Well do not keep me in torture, I beg of you.

VILLAMOUR.

The person now with your mistress is not what she takes him for!

F 2 FLO-

FLORINDA.

What is he then?

VILLAMOUR.

My fervant.

FLORINDA.

And——————(*with agitation.*)

VILLAMOUR.

I myfelf am——————*Villamour!*

FLORINDA.

Ah!

VILLAMOUR.

I hoped under this difguife to know your lady more perfectly before I declared myfelf——but the ftratagem has entangled me——I diflike the woman I ought to be married to, and love the *maid* who fhould in me only have found a *new mafter.*

FLORINDA.

I'll keep my own council——he fhall not know me yet:
(*Afide*)

VILLAMOUR.

How would you have me act?—Your miftrefs has fuch a vulgar tafte, that fhe's actually enamoured of my footman; and if I do not inftantly prevent it, the father will confent to their nuptials——What am I to do?

FLORINDA.

Your cafe is a moft extraordinary one indeed, Sir.—— But firft of all I requeft your pardon for whatever has appeared difrefpectful or improper in my paft behavour to you.

VILLAMOUR.

Do not fpeak of it, it will only recall the diftance between us, aud make me more wretched and difconfolate.

FLORINDA.

But I permit you, Sir, to revoke all the kind affectionate declarations made me, as I would not have you let down your dignity, on a *poor fervant* like me.

VIL-

VILLAMOUR.

But though I cannot unite my fate with yours, Letty, (since I am not fortunate enough to gain your love) yet it is some consolation that you declared you did not hate me.

FLORINDA:

Hist——I hear someby coming——have a little patience with regard to your servant——matters are not so desperate as you think——we will meet again immediately, and consult how to relieve you from this perplexing affair.

VILLAMOUR.

You shall entirely direct me.

(Exit Villamour.

Enter Young Meanwell.

YOUNG MEANWELL.

So I have caught you again, sister, and perhaps almost in the same situation——Pray were you teaching the young man his prayers again?

FLORINDA.

You may now say whatever you please, brother, for I have *such* agreeable news to tell you.

YOUNG MEONWELL.

What about?

FLORINDA.

Skipwell is not Skipwell—nor Villamour Villemour.

YOUNG MEANWELL.

I do not understand you—you speak in riddles.

FLORINDA.

I had it just now from himself.

YOUNG MEANWELL.

From whom pray? or what is it, I cannot comprehend you?

FLORINDA.

Come, my father must be informed of it——I shall have occasion for your assistance too——I must now concert a plan to secure the heart I before rejected——and request, brother

brother, that you will be very fecret, and not mention a word of it.

YOUNG MEANWELL.

O! never fear, I'll be fecret enough, for I cannot divulge what I do not know.

FLORINDA

Come along, brother, let us lofe no time ; there never was any thing more propitious or more pleafing than this is. [Exit baftily.

YOUNG MEANWELL.

I fee that *Villamour* has thrown off the mafk at laft. Here he comes—I'll have fome fport with him.

Enter Villamour.

YOUNG MEANWELL.

Stay, Skipwell, a word with you.

VILLAMOUR.

What would you pleafe to fay, Sir.

YOUNG MEANWELL.

You have made love to our maid, Letty, I underftand.

VILLAMOUR.

How could one be in company with her, and refrain from it, Sir?

YOUNG MEANWELL.

Does fhe receive you kindly ?

VILLAMOUR.

You would not have me fo ungallant as to tell, Sir— But fuppofe *fhe bad* a partiality for me, how does it concern *you*, Sir.

YOUNG MEANWELL.

A partiality for you ! a fine ftory truly——No——no— fhe could not have fuch a defpicable opinion of herfelf as to look at one *fo much beneath her bopes*.

VILLAMOUR.

So much beneath her hopes !——

YOUNG MEANWELL.

Yes, for I'll condefcend to *tell* you, Sir, that I have a very *bonourable regard* and *brotherly affection* for this girl,

and

and she knows it, and it is her own fault if she remains long single, let my father take it as he will.

VILLAMOUR.

O, this accounts for the high and ambitious tone my lady talks in—(*Aside*)

YOUNG MEANWELL.

I therefore cannot brook a lover of your rank in her train.

VILLAMOUR.

Faith ! I believe you, Sir, for I am not satisfied with a rival like *you*, as you must of course bear away the prize —if she loves you in return.

YOUNG MEANWELL.

Loves me in return ;' do you imagine I am not deserving of it ?

VILLAMOUR.

O, yes, Sir, but you do not expect praise from *one you* suppose your rival?

YOUNG MEANWELL.

Pray who am I speaking to ? You seem a very conceited kind of a gentleman.

VILLAMOUR.

Speaking to, Sir—to Skipwell.

YOUNG MEANWELL.

Well, I desire I may never hear or see any more of your attempts on *Letty's* affections—if I do, your master must correct you, or you will find me a different person to deal with.   [*Exit Young Meanwell.*

VILLAMOUR.

Must I bear these repeated injuries, and have both my honour and my love insulted? Yet I think this attachment cannot be mutual :—however *Letty* shall clear up all doubts, and one way or other disentangle me from this labyrinth of anxiety, hope and perplexity.   [*Exit*

Scene

Scene changes to another Apartment in Meanwell's House.

Enter Old Meanwell and Letty.

LETTY.

Sir, you told me you gave Villamour up entirely to my management——I took you at your word, and have now taught him to hop after me like a *pet magpie* ; but do you think my miſtreſs will reſign her pretenſions to him.

OLD MEANWELL.

O yes ; ſhe bids me tell you that ſhe has given up all right and title to him, as you took ſo much pains to train him to your own liking.

LETTY.

And have I really your permiſſion to marry him, Sir ?

OLD MEANWELL.

Have not I given it already ?——You have my conſent without *his* aſking it——but I muſt lay one reſtriction on you to exculpate ourſelves——I inſiſt upon it, that you will give him a hint who you are.

LETTY.

O Lord, Sir, if I give him the leaſt hint, that (as my lover himſelf wou'd ſay) will be entirely ' *letting the cat out of the bag.*'

OLD MEANWELL.

But you know he follows you about like a *pet magpie*— and he is ſo much under your command that I deſire you will do it.

LETTY.

Well, for Heaven's ſake retire, Sir——my enamorato's to meet me——this you know is the finiſhing ſtroke to make my fortune——ſo leave me a clear ſtage, and fair play.

OLD MEANWELL.

Acquit yourſelf handſomely then.

LETTY.

Never fear, Sir, and now compleat my conqueſt !——

                 (*Exit Meanwell.*

—What a lucky girl thou art, Letty—O I ſhall run wild

with

with my good fortune, and fo outſhine the world in dreſs, equipage, routes, maſquerades, balls, and I don't know what !———But here comes my lover———

Enter Skipwell.

SKIPWELL.

Have I at length found you, my dove?——Ah! as the play fay—'Was it not unkind to leave me like a *turkey droping*, all alone?'

LETTY.

Rather illiterate——but no matter, his fortune makes amends—(*Aſide*)——I am ſure, Sir, it is not my wiſh to be abſent from you—for I have drooped like a *moultring Canary bird*, ſince we parted.

SKIPWELL.

Oh! you are ſweeter and dearer to me—*than molaſſes to a Yankee Doodle.*

LETTY.

And you are the very honey-comb, currant-jelly, and marmalade of my affection.

SKIPWELL.

Oh, the delicious words !——do let my lips ſmack them up from yours———
(*Sings*) I'm brim-full of love, and you're all over charms.
And like a lad of wax I muſt melt in your arms.
(*Kiſſing her*)

LETTY.

Oh! fye, Sir——you are ſo *preſſing* upon one——

SKIPWELL.

O that is true—pray, Miſs, accept this *bucket* of myrtle.
(*Preſenting ſome myrtle*)

LETTY.

'Tis vaſtly pretty, Sir.

SKIPWELL.

And like yourſelf, Ma'am, the more you *ſqueeze* it, the ſweeter it is.

LETTY.

Oh! Lord, Sir !

G SLIP.

SKIPWELL.

Egad, as she is in so coming a humour, I had better
for fear of a difcovery——Sweet, fugar plumb of affection, I am dying with impatience at the delay of our happinefs——What fay you to a private match! I'll go and
marry you inftantly, for I am *broiling* on Cupid's gridiron.

LETTY.

I'll ftrike while the iron is hot——How he jumps into
my wifhes!—(*Afide*)

SKIPWELL.

Well, my primrofe, whàt fay you?

LETTY.

Why, Sir, if I thought you would not confider me *too
forward*.

SKIPWELL.

Too forward, my tit moufe, not in the leaft, I fhould
hate you if you was *too backward*——In the name of love,
then, let the prieft get before the lawyer; for I know one
at hand, who will tack us together before you can fay trap-
ftick.

LETTY.

Oh, la, Sir, *but what fhall I fay to my papa?*

SKIPWELL.

Oh! what's always faid upon thefe occafions, Honey!
We will come back and fall upon our marrow-bones, afk
pardon, and fay that our love was fo violent we could not
help it.

LETTY.

Well, on one condition, I'll confent.

SKIPWELL.

Name it quickly, then, fugar-candy of my foul——

LETTY.

That you will keep our marriage fecret, 'till I give you
leave to mention it.

SKIPWELL.

Silent as a dumb man——Come, then, my girl—we
will fly to Father Tackum——I'll throw my commiffion
at your feet. [*Exeunt*
Scene

Scene a Room in Meanwell's House.

Enter Old and Young Meanwell and Florinda.

FLORINDA.

If I did not love Villamour you muſt own I ſhould be very ungrateful.

OLD MEANWELL.

So you got a little *out* of him in the converſation you had together?

YOUNG MEANWELL.

No, he was too crafty, and never thrown off his guard, though I endeavoured to put his temper to the teſt.

OLD MEANWELL.

Well, I am very glad that he is the dupe of his own ſtratagem——nothing however can be more flattering to him than the diſcretion with which you, *Flora*, have hitherto acted

YOUNG MEANWELL.

But how far has he proceeded, Siſter; I hope his jealouſy of me will not have any adverſe conſequences?

FLORINDA.

I have not the leaſt reaſon to be diſſatisfied with him;— and as to you, the next interview muſt bring about an explanation.

OLD MEANWELL.

Why, girl, you have not vanity enough to expect that he'll be ſo deſperate as to offer you his hand in your preſent character?

FLORINDA,

Yes, Sir, elſe he never ſhall have mine——but I know we are deſtined for each other——it was a match regiſtered above, and muſt be accompliſhed here;—what obligations I owe you, Sir, for indulging my ſcheme——Villamour can never think of the ſtory without loving me, and I'll never talk of it, without loving him——it was laying the foundation of our happineſs for life——it was the moſt propitious contrivance of chance—the moſt *lucky deception.*

G 2　　　　　YOUNG MEAN

YOUNG MEANWELL,

Hey day! Sifter, how you run on, what a flood of eloquence.

OLD MEANWELL.

Well, if *you* end as you began, it will be the moft delightful entertainment to all parties.

FLORINDA,

You will fee that immediately——I tell you Villamour is conquered, and I have him in my chains.

OLD MEANWELL.

And they are *golden* ones, which is more than he expected; but I begin to pity his fufferings, and wifh him relieved from his folicitude.

FLORINDA.

But I muft be witnefs to more before I difplay my compaffion.

YOUNG MEANWELL.

To fee prudence lofe the victory in the conflict—— Eh, Flora!

OLD MEANWELL.

As much as to fay that he fhould be fenfible of his folly and difgrace, and yet fubmit to your fafcination!——What a prefumptuous arrogance of felf-love!

FLORINDA.

It is the felf-love of a woman, father, and that never varies from its object——but go to your pofts, and you'll fee how I will compleat my conqueft.

(Exeunt feverally.

Scene changes to another Apartment in Meanwell's Houfe.

Enter Villamour and Skipwell.

VILLAMOUR.

Well, Skipwell, have you feen the lady and difcovered yourfelf as I ordered you.

SKIPWELL.

As I have fworn fecrecy to my dulcinea about our marriage, I muft diffemble a little—(*Afide*)——O yes, Sir,
I told

I told her I was not what I feemed, that my real name was *Skipwell*—that I was only a poor foldier, and occafionally your footman.——Very well, my lad, faid fhe, every body has fome rank and uniform on the ftage of life. —Your livery cofts you nothing—fo much the better for us both.

What a ridiculous ftory you are telling me.

O, Sir, you may lead a woman with a cobweb though you cannot drag her with a cable; and I have done it to fome purpofe, for we are going to be tethered directly.

VILLAMOUR.

What! with the family's confent.

SKIPWELL.

Marry come up, and what difgrace to her family, pray?

VILLAMOUR.

You are a very impudent fellow, Skipwell!

SKIPWELL.

And if it was not for a little *impudence a modeft man* could not thrive in this world, Sir.—I purfued my way and found it.

VILLAMOUR.

It is not poffible;—I will therefore go myfelf and acquaint Mr. Meanwell how matters are fituated.

SKIPWELL.

Who! old decency, my father-in-law?——O, we have him under our thumb, I affure you——he is a very good natured, jolly, honeft cock, and has given his confent already.

VILLAMOUR.

Pfhaw! you are a blockhead——Have you feen Letty lately?

SKIPWELL.

Letty!—not that I recollect——but I have other fifh to fry, and above taking notice of fuch low cattle as waiting-maids——I have given up that kind of game to you, Sir.

VILLAMOUR.

Vanity or love has turned the fellow's brain, I believe.

SKIP-

SKIPWELL.

'You are free and eafy; however when I am married and fettled, I will be glad to fee you at my houfe in town——and hope whenever you vifit England, you will make me your home, and that we will live together as old friends and new acquaintances.

VILLAMOUR.

You do me a great deal of honour. Sir.

SKIPWELL.

But I fee your waiting-maid there at the end of the gallery——perhaps you wifh to fee her—for I muft to my love ———— .

Exit finging—" I kifs'd and prattled with *fifty five* maids, &c."

VILLAMOUR.

What an original he is—But now for Letty.

Enter Florinda.

VILLAMOUR.

Stay, Letty, ftay—I intreat you ftay—I have fome-thing very ferious to fay to you.

FLORINDA.

To me, Sir?

VILLAMOUR.

It troubles me to leave you without convincing you I do not think myfelf to blame in fo doing.

FLORINDA.

Why need you juftify yourfelf to *me*, Sir,

VILLAMOUR.

It is my wifh to be undeceived——but Young Mean-well loves you;—he told me fo, and with an *honourable*, *brotherly affection* !

FLORINDA.

Very true ————

VILLAMOUR.

And I conclude you are fenfible of his paffion from the indifference with which you treat *me*.

FLO-

FLORINDA.

I muft own I love him equal to myfelf, but I never can be *bis* wife, and he knows it.

VILLAMOUR.

What a contradiction !——Explain yourfelf, I conjure you, and at once tell me your fituation, as my happinefs is ftaked upon it.

FLORINDA.

Tell a man that is leaving me.

VILLAMOUR.

I will not leave you——I can never leave you.—But fince you know I adore you above every woman upon earth. Give me then poffeffion of a hand and heart I value above the world.

FLORINDA.

What in fpite of degrading yourfelf—in fpite of your father's difpleafure !

VILLAMOUR.

He will forgive me the inftant he has feen you——as to the world's opinion, my happinefs will fmile at its malice, and your worth be an antidote againft the venom of its cenfure.

Enter Old and Young Meanwell.

OLD MEANWELL.

' Againft the venom of its cenfure.'

OLD and YOUNG MEANWELL.

Ha! ha! ha! ha!

OLD MEANWELL.

We have heard it all, not a fyllable has efcaped us—I find you have not waited for my confent.

Enter Letty and Skipwell.

YOUNG MEANWELL.

Did not we tell you it would come to this?

FLORINDA.

Oh, my deareft father !

VILLAMOUR.

What do I hear——*her* father !

SKIP.

SKIPWELL.

And what do *I* hear——her father !——(*Aside.*)

VILLAMOUR.

You, her father, Sir—— ——

OLD'MEANWELL.

Yes, Villamour——the fame ftratagem, the fame *deception* was contrived by mutual chance againft each other.

LETTY.

Villamour ! and who the duce have I married ?—(*Aside.*)

SKIPWELL.

(*Going up to Letty*)——Who the devil are you, Ma'am?

LETTY.

And who the duce are *you*, Sir ?—(*To Skipwell.*)

VILLAMOUR.

This is my footman—Madam—(*to Letty.*)

FLORINDA.

And this is my waiting-maid Sir ?——(*to Skipwell.*)

LETTY.

O, how my fine hopes are vanifhed !

SKIPWELL.

Zounds ! but what a tumble I have got !

VILLAMOUR.

Come, Skipwell, no more of this——but as you and
Mrs. Letty have been acting for us on this occafion, I
fhall endeavour to reward you to your fatisfaction.

FLORINDA.

Yes, our good fortune fhall contribute to theirs——
they muft drrop their grandeur and titles, but they fhall
amply experience my kindnefs.

SKIPWELL.

Then, Mrs. Rib, I take you with all my foul——" for
Skipwell's himfelf again."

LETTY.

And, Bone of *my* Bone, I am yours with all my heart—
and you know we fwore it, ' in fpite of all the changes and
chequers of this immortal life.'

OLD

OLD MEANWELL.

Well, Flora, did not I tell you, that Villamour would
be the man of your choice at laſt?

FLORINDA.

You told me but the truth indeed, ſir.

YOUNG MEANWELL.

Will Villamour forget the affronts I gave to Skipwell?

VILLAMOUR.

I not only forgive but thank you. (*takes his hand.*) But
what delights me moſt are the proofs I gave you, Florinda,
of the purity and diſintereſtedneſs of my paſſion.

FLORINDA.

And you may judge of the value I ſet upon your heart,
by the means I took to gain it.

VILLAMOUR.

Here, however, my dear Florinda, let us jointly re-
nounce all diſguiſe and diſſimulation ; and let us both, for
the future, by mutual franknefs and ſincerity, endeavour
to atone to each other for our mutual deception.

F   I   N   I   S.

Lately Publiſhed.

I. MATCH FOR A WIDOW, a Comic Opera, by the Author of this Piece, 1s. 6d.

II. JULIA, OT THE ITALIAN LOVER, a Tragedy, by R. Jephſon, Eſq. 1s. 6d.

III. THE FIRST FLOOR, a Farce, by Mr. Cobb, 1s.

IV. THE SULTAN, OR A PEEP INTO THE SERAGLIO, a Farce, 6d.

V. ENGLISH READINGS, a Comic Piece, 1s.

www.ingramcontent.com/pod-product-compliance
Lightning Source LLC
Chambersburg PA
CBHW022200020726
47496CB00008B/2812